Blueprint For Value

52 Habits to Discover and Strengthen
Your Personal Worth

Jeff Koziatek

Requests for permission to reproduce any part of this work should be emailed to the publisher at:
CoreAuthenticityPress.com

This publication is designed to provide accurate and authoritative information in regard to the subject matter covered. It is sold with the understanding that the publisher is not engaged in rendering legal, accounting, or other professional service. If legal advice or other expert assistance is required, the services of a competent professional person should be sought.

Blueprint for Value: 52 Habits to Discover and Strengthen Your Personal Worth/Jeff Koziatek

First edition

ISBN-13: 978-1-7326913-0-8

1 - Self-Help SEL023000, SEL031000
2 - Body, Mind & Spirit OCC019000

Cover art by Stephanie Kennedy
Author photo by Linda Rivard Photography

Printed in the United States of America

10 9 8 7 6 5 4 3 2 1

To my wife Brandi

Who loves me for me, not my successes, circumstances, or failures. I'm so grateful to be sharing life with you.
With all my love.

To my sons Cale and Aiden

Who inspire me daily to live a bold, authentic life. I love you both and will always be on your team, fighting alongside you, mentoring you, and cheering you on as you both pursue your dreams.

To my parents

Who stood up for me and encouraged me to pursue what was in my heart. Thank you.

Contents

Acknowledgments   vii
Introduction   ix
How to read this book   xii

Chapter 1 - Engage   1
    #1 - Foundation Values   2
    #2 - Dig   3
    #3 - Dreams & Purpose   4
    #4 - Awareness   5
    #5 - Know the Enemy   6
    #6 - Expectations   7
    #7 - Be Authentic   8
    #8 - Be Kind to Yourself   9
    #9 - Listen   10
    #10 - Grace of Gray   11
    #11 - Dead Weight   12
    #12 - Focus   13
    #13 - Pacing   14

Chapter 2 - Equip   15
    #14 - Sleep   16
    #15 - Fuel   17
    #16 - Body Care   18
    #17 - Posture   19
    #18 - Smile   20
    #19 - Take Out the Trash   21
    #20 - Stack Pebbles   22
    #21 - Responsibility   23
    #22 - Knowledge   24
    #23 - Attitude   25
    #24 - Routine   26
    #25 - Environment   27
    #26 - Fellowship   28

Chapter 3 - Empower   29
    #27 - Flexibility   30
    #28 - High Hands   31
    #29 - All In   32
    #30 - Weeding   33
    #31 - On Time   34
    #32 - Airplane Mode   35
    #33 - Ask   36
    #34 - Scribble   37
    #35 - Today's Best   38
    #36 - Enough   39
    #37 - Break   40
    #38 - Jump!   41
    #39 - Mistakes   42

Chapter 4 - Encourage   43
    #40 - Firefighter   44
    #41 - Not me   45
    #42 - Affirmations   46
    #43 - Self-Respect   47
    #44 - Forgive Yourself   48
    #45 - Pay Once   49
    #46 - Lens   50
    #47 - Emotions   51
    #48 - It's the Audition!   52
    #49 - Yet   53
    #50 - Celebrate   54
    #51 - Record   55
    #52 - #WashYourBrain   56

A final note from Jeff   57
Next steps   59
About the author   61
But wait, there's more!   62
Notes   63

Acknowledgments

This book exists because of a fantastic team of individuals who have been honest with me, provided me opportunities, cared for me, encouraged me, and believed in me when I didn't believe in myself. Thank you to:

• My editing team: Lisa Brown, Katie Chatfield, Cory Edwards, Stephanie Kennedy, Brandi Koziatek, Mary Pohlman, John Wherle, and Mark Williams. I am an external processor, and your feedback was invaluable.

• My coach Jeff Arthur, who shined a light in the darkness, supported me, encouraged me, and equipped me for success.

• Steve Hughes, who took me under his wing and helped me find my footing as a speaker.

• Robyn Hatcher, Dawn Mushill, and Bob Pacanovsky for your encouragement to write this book.

• Cleveland Mack, for the cover design, Stephanie Kennedy for amazing cover art! (https://www.linkedin.com/in/stephanie-kennedy-design/) and Linda Rivard for cover photography (http://www.lindarivardphotography.com),

• My family, for believing in me and giving me time to pursue my passion and write this book.

• God, for His pursuit, mercy and love.

Introduction

We must see value in ourselves before we can see it in others. Our personal worth, our value, forms the foundation of our thoughts, behaviors, decisions and relationships, both personal and professional.

We all have intrinsic value that never changes; however, our perception of it *can* and *does* change. Throughout this book, I will be referring to the perception of value as a Personal Worth Account (PWA) that can be grown or depleted through deposits or withdrawals.

When our PWA is low, we can easily:

- hide from our feelings in addiction(s)
- view ourselves as worthless
- treat others as if they are worthless
- protect and justify our external value
- fight to earn more external value
- avoid situations where external value can be lost or stolen
- inflate our perceived value
- flaunt our perceived value
- avoid associations with people we see as having less value than ourselves
- judge others
- spend time in constant comparison
- compete when there is no competition
- lose hope
- see everything as someone else's fault

Don't panic! There is another way. Your worth is not linked to a circumstance, success, failure or appearance. As I mentioned, your value is internal. It never changes. It cannot be lost, stolen or increased.

I want to help you experience more of your internal value by changing how you see yourself. You are holding a compilation of 52 uncommon, common sense habits that can help you build your Personal Worth Account (PWA). They have been organized into four categories: Engage, Equip, Empower, Encourage.

Engage *with yourself to discover the "why" behind your actions, thoughts, and feelings.*

Equip *yourself with the right tools for the right job.*

Empower *yourself with opportunities to lead, succeed, or fail without judgment.*

Encourage *yourself to continue forward and make course corrections along the way.*

You have immeasurable value simply because you are alive.

This book is not meant to be an exhaustive, deep dive into any one particular habit. There are incredible books out there on mindset, presence, attitude, choice, diet, and purpose. Rather, this book should be a field guide, serving as a:

- Reminder of a habit you forgot
- Refresher of why a habit is important
- Guide to a new habit you might adopt

Use *Blueprint* to help discover and strengthen your PWA.

How to read this book

Blueprint for Value was designed as a quick reference guide. Although it is not intended to be read cover to cover, there is no wrong way to read this book.

- Take your time, spend a week developing one habit.

- Flip through at random and surprise yourself.

- When you feel overwhelmed and stressed, use this book to find a habit that will get you back on track.

- Lacking focus or having difficulty making decisions? Dig into your foundation with *Engage*.

- When you don't feel adequately prepared, look over *Equip*.

- Dragging your feet? Are excuses holding you back? Motivate yourself with *Empower*.

- If you are facing criticism and challenges, refresh yourself with *Encourage*.

The habits do not build on each other. You can begin this book in Chapter 1 or 4, or anywhere in between.

This book is here for you. Pull yourself off the battlefield, remember your worth, grab some habits and then get back out there! The world needs your unique perspective and talents.

You are worth it.

You have value.

Chapter 1

Engage

Be honest about what's going on with you: your circumstances, your opportunities, your strengths, your resources, your challenges, and your time. Find out what drives your actions, thoughts, and feelings.

Engage through discovery and action.

#1 - Foundation Values

What you value impacts your decisions.

Whether you are aware of them or not, you know when you do something that grates against your core values. Acting against them erodes your confidence, makes you feel "off" and lowers your feeling of personal worth.

Know what you stand for and what you stand against. That knowledge can be a guiding compass. Take time to examine your core values and write them down. You'll find yourself better able to make confident, sometimes bold choices.

Each decision, made in accordance with your values, will become easier to make and add deposits to your Personal Worth Account (PWA).

Takeaway

Your core values are the foundation for everything you do. Your values are a personal compass pointing the way to your future.

#2 - Dig

To deal with the symptom, tackle the root.

Accepting life's circumstances at face value is easy. We might say, "It is what it is," or "This is just how I am." It can be painful to dig into the past and ask, "Why are things this way?" or even, "Why am I this way?"

Are your thoughts, beliefs and behaviors serving you? If not, change them. Ask yourself, "Where does this belief/thought come from? What happened to trigger this behavior?"

Nurture the roots that serve you and remove the roots that don't.

Digging down to the roots of your thoughts, beliefs and behaviors can broaden your self-knowledge and grow your PWA.

Takeaway

Change starts with the root. Get dirty. Be brave. Take an honest look, dig deep, and ask, "Who, what, when, where, why, and how?"

#3 - Dreams & Purpose

Everyone needs a dream, a clear purpose.

It's easy to let life happen to you when you lack purpose and have no dream to chase. You can easily spend large amounts of energy pursuing another person's goals. You can be tempted to move against your core values as you work hard to achieve someone else's purpose. When you don't know your own purpose, you can often feel exhausted, drained, and depressed. Times likes these can leave you vulnerable and more open to the power of persuasion.

Dreams and purpose keep you alive. They give you direction. They can also give you the permission to stand on your values. Pursuing your passion can energize you, grow your confidence and build your PWA.

As your feeling of personal worth increases, so does your energy to pursue your dreams and live a boldly authentic life. They create a sustainable loop—feeding each other.

Takeaway

Don't be afraid to dream. Dreams are key for living a life of purpose and joy.

#4 - Awareness

How do the people in your life affect you?

Are your current surroundings beating you down? Do you call toxic people "friends?" Do you allow "negative" circumstances to keep you from living out your values and dreams? Are you allowing factors outside your control to shape your sense of personal worth?

You cannot always control what happens to you, but you can always choose how you respond.

Stop, observe, take inventory, and seek an outside perspective to make sure you didn't miss anything. Don't be blind to your environment, allowing it to sweep you downstream and drain your PWA. Surround yourself with people that love and inspire you. If they aren't encouraging you, make changes whenever possible. If you can't make a change, remember that *you* are in control of how you respond.

Takeaway

Your circumstances and other people do not define you. What factors outside of your control are impacting how you see yourself?

#5 - Know the Enemy

Known and unknown fear can stop you.

Whether you're aware of them or not, fear and distraction can diminish your PWA. They can be blind spots that carry enormous weight and dramatically affect the course of your life.

It's easy to pick up fear from your life influencers, environment, and media only to unwillingly adopt them as your own. Similarly, distractions can pop-up and grab your attention. Suddenly you're playing a Whac-A-Mole game that steals your time and energy.

Take time to understand your fears. Listen to them carefully and respond to them with the truth. Naming your enemy—your worries, distractions, doubts—gives you the opportunity to engage, respond, and grow, instead of losing ground and depleting your PWA.

Takeaway

Doubts, distractions, and fears can act like an invisible chain, keeping you from your dreams. Take stock of any that might be holding you back and destroy them with truth.

#6 - Expectations

What must happen for you to feel (<u>fill in the blank</u>)?

We all want to feel successful, happy, loved, and confident. When we don't feel that way, our PWA starts to drop. What conditions need to be met for you to feel those things?

When you link your expectations to another person's actions (or other factors beyond your control), you give up accountability and become the victim. You relinquish power over your feelings to someone or something else.

Take back your power. Hold yourself responsible instead of someone else. Alter your expectations to be dependent solely on things you can control and watch your PWA and confidence increase.

Takeaway

Take control of your feelings—shift your expectations from external to internal factors— things you can control. Take responsibility or you will forever play the victim.

#7 - Be Authentic

It is ok to be you.

When you feel worthless, it's easy to hide behind a mask of "significance." Pretending to be someone you are not simply to gain the acceptance of others can be enticing—but at what cost?

Wearing a mask robs you of precious time and energy as you focus on keeping up appearances while sacrificing genuine human connection, vulnerability, and loyalty.

When you drop the mask and embrace who you are, your problem solving capacity increases. You have more time, your energy level rises, and you make more deposits in your PWA.

Bold authenticity can give you the sustainable power to do what you've been put on Earth to do.

Takeaway

Drop the mask. Be you and watch your confidence grow. The world needs you to be your unique self. There is only one you—and you're it.

#8 - Be Kind to Yourself

You are a person, not an object or a mistake.

No one is perfect. Everyone makes mistakes. It's easy to punish yourself for making mistakes. You might even be encouraged to identify by your mistakes. Unfortunately, this type of punishment takes away your humanity and can drain your PWA.

Great news! Mistakes do not define you. Although you cannot eliminate errors, you can take steps to minimize their effects and reduce how often they occur. What you do after you make a mistake is critical.

You are a person. You will have good days and bad. Enjoy the good days. Be kind to yourself on the bad days.

When you choose to learn instead of giving up, you affirm your self-worth. Your mistakes no longer consume you.

Takeaway

After making a mistake, give yourself mercy and the opportunity to grow.

#9 - Listen

Stop the "busy." Be still. Listen to your heart.

Hundreds of messages come at you daily. Life can get busy and cluttered with other voices and other agendas. It's easy to get caught in the "busy" and blindly follow those outside voices— voices that tell you what you should want, that you don't have enough, or what you should and shouldn't care about. This can lead to unhealthy competition, comparison, and judgment. These voices can also move you away from your core values.

You have a voice. You have values. You are worthy.

Turn off the screen. Turn down the music. Spend some time alone. Be still and listen. No judgment, just observation. What is in your heart? Listening can be a great tool to affirm your worth and make deposits in your PWA.

Takeaway

Take a moment. Slow down. Listen to your heart. Stop comparing. See yourself through your own eyes.

#10 - Grace of Gray

Perfection isn't as important as showing up.

The perfectionist mindset is destined for failure and unhappiness. It provides fertile ground for shame, guilt, and worry. It says, "There is no gray, only black and white. Good or bad. All or nothing. Right or wrong. Pass or fail."

Making an attempt, regardless of the outcome, is valuable. Mistakes can be helpful tools for growth. Give yourself the grace to make mistakes and acknowledge growth when it happens.

Avoid using the unattainable mindset of perfection. Nurture a mindset of moving towards your goal with the flexibility to grow, change, and make mistakes. Positive momentum can make significant deposits in your PWA.

Takeaway

Perfection is unreachable. Drop the measuring stick and the heavy weight of self-judgment. Give yourself permission to show up and learn.

#11 - Dead Weight

Drop responsibility for another person's thoughts, feelings, or actions.

You are responsible for showing up and giving what you can. Beyond that, it's up to other people to receive what you have shared and choose their response. That's their responsibility— not yours.

A comedian's job is to make people laugh, but it's an equation with three variables: the performance, the audience, and the environment. The performer can do his or her best (and can often have some control over the environment), but the audience can choose to engage or not. It's their choice. Taking on 100% responsibility for the audience's response makes them objects to manipulate or obstacles to overcome.

Don't rob people of their humanity by assuming responsibility for what they do, feel, think, or believe. That is not your burden.

Takeaway

Do not weigh yourself down with responsibility that is not (and never was) yours to carry.

#12 - Focus

What are you looking at?

Your focus determines your direction. Where are you focusing your time and energy?

The object you focus on takes top priority. Items in your periphery are a distant second. Anything you can't see is quickly forgotten, if you even notice it at all.

Do you pour your time, energy and resources into reinforcing your problems? Or do you look for solutions? Are you focused on the symptom or the root? Do you miss the good because of an intense focus on the bad?

Your focus impacts your perception of the world, your growth, and your ability to solve problems. How do you choose to see the world?

Takeaway

Acknowledge the negative and focus on the positive. It will build your PWA and you'll feel more energized to tackle the task at hand.

#13 - Pacing

Slow down. You don't need to rush.

We want to "keep up with the Joneses" and prove our worth. Comparison and seeking external value can cause us to rush through life and glorify "busy."

When you rush, you can miss essential details. Your checklists can become consuming, and your journey can become a grind.

When you move too fast, you can lose sight of your values and your motivating WHY. As your purpose becomes clouded, what you do and how you do it can become tedious and steal your focus. In fact, your purpose can evaporate while you seek to stay busy.

Don't drown yourself in busyness. Take some time for yourself. You deserve it.

Takeaway

Take time to remember your WHY: your purpose and what you value. You owe it to your dreams and yourself not to rush through life.

14

Chapter 2

Equip

Prepare yourself for success by acquiring and refining your tool kit. It's all about having the right tool for the right job.

Equip yourself with a firm foundation, the correct tools, and a supportive team.

#14 - Sleep

Sleep for productivity and focus.

Sleep is the foundation from which you start your day. Sleep affects your energy level along with your ability to focus and listen. Sleep can sharpen your perception and allow you to effectively give and receive feedback. Everything you do begins from a place of rest, but it's often the first thing you sacrifice.

Take a second and think, how much sleep am I getting? Am I fully rested or am I running on fumes?

Establishing a routine sleep schedule (same bedtime, same wake-up time), getting adequate amounts of sleep, avoiding screens right before bed, and writing down your thoughts to quiet your mind are great ways to improve your sleep and grow your PWA.

Takeaway

Sleep is more than just resting. It's the backbone of life. Sleep to be more awake.

#15 - Fuel

You are what you eat.

You need power to run. The food you consume can strengthen you and improve your efficiency or slow you down and cloud your judgment. Are you eating junk food but expecting to function at peak performance?

A simple food change can have a tremendous impact on:

* Your mind's ability to think clearly

* Your body's ability to repair itself and function properly

* Your perspective on your circumstances.

What's in your diet?

Takeaway

Eat foods that propel your body rather than slow it down. Food is more than just filling or a good taste—it's necessary fuel to keep your body running.

#16 - Body Care

Pay attention to what your body needs.

You only get one body, so why not take care of it? Listen to your body. Does it need rest? Does something need a tune-up? Do you need some TLC?

Like your car needs regular maintenance, your body needs attention, too. Stretch it, strengthen it, fuel it, and care for it.

Abusing your body by ignoring pain, being careless and not tending to issues as they arise can cause consequences beyond physical aches and pains. When you are in pain, or your body doesn't function properly, it can distract you, slow down your production, deplete your resources, and alter your perception of the past, present, and the future.

A body that is properly maintained can be a reliable foundation, will perform on demand, and will not drain your PWA.

Takeaway

Take care of your body, and your body will take care of you.

#17 - Posture

Assume the position of the feeling you want.

Your posture affects your emotions. You've heard the phrase "dress for the job you want, not the job you have." Apply that concept by adopting the posture of the feeling you want, not the feeling you have. Let your body lead.

Slouching, dragging your feet, and avoiding eye contact can produce feelings of depression, inadequacy, or an "I don't care" attitude.

Keeping your shoulders back with your chest up and your head held high can build confidence even if you don't feel confident at first. Sit up straight. Stand tall. Use your body to help change your mind.

Move with confidence to gain confidence.

Takeaway

You can change your feelings by improving your posture.

#18 - Smile

A smile is powerful, inexpensive medicine!

Smiling releases chemicals in the brain that make you feel good.

Even when you are sad, a simple smile can change your attitude. This is not about being fake or living in denial. A smile can be a personal mood changer, another tool to gain control over your emotions.

You can experience these benefits any time. You don't even have to see your smile. Smile while driving or looking in a mirror. You can smile when you're alone or smile in a group.

Use a smile as often as you like—it never runs out! And it's contagious! You can share generously.

Takeaway

How do you want to feel? Change how you feel with a smile.

#19 - Take Out the Trash

Let go of old baggage.

Leave yesterday's hurts and mistakes in the past. They can take up valuable space in your head, and if you hold on to them long enough, they will start to define you. You are not your circumstances, failures, or mistakes! Let them go and forgive past wrongs.

You are also not a calendar. Empty your brain of clutter. Write down to-do lists. Keep track of things you need to remember in a notebook or app. Empty the trashcan. Organize and simplify as you unclutter your mind.

Your brain can only hold so much at one time. If you are full of negative "trash," you won't be able to remember the positives from the past or present. Not to mention, it will be difficult to see potential positives in the future.

Takeaway

Take only what you need to survive. What extra baggage are you carrying?

#20 - Stack Pebbles

Momentum from "small" wins can create a big victory.

Don't eat the elephant all at once! Break it down. You might not be able to move a mountain now, but maybe you could move a rock or stack a pebble. Stack enough pebbles and you have a wall. Move enough rocks and eventually you have a pyramid or mountain.

Remembering and celebrating a series of wins can alter your self-perception. You may start to feel more confident and realize that you do have something to offer the world.

Achieving small goals can build personal trust. The more you trust yourself, the more sense of personal worth you experience. Keep stacking pebbles and watch your PWA grow.

Takeaway

Every journey begins with a step. What simple step can you take today? Look to succeed through small, easily achievable goals in order to reach your big dream. Rome wasn't built in a day.

#21 - Responsibility

Do what you say you're going to do.

Show up when you say you're going to show up. Stick with your commitments. Let your word be true, even when no one is looking. In fact, you get bonus points when no one is looking!

Your worth is not your word, but keeping your word can improve how you feel about yourself. Hold yourself accountable to the rules you set. Personal accountability can make significant deposits in your PWA.

Prove to yourself that you can be trusted. Trust builds confidence. Confidence is a bankable asset. Reallocate that confidence as needed.

Takeaway

Build a foundation of self-accountability. Be responsible for you. Grow your PWA by sticking to your word—public or private.

#22 - Knowledge

You are never too old to learn something new.

Learning helps maintain neuroplasticity. Running the system clears the cobwebs and keeps your brain functioning in peak condition. Leave the gates to knowledge forever open.

Not only is learning good for performance, some studies have shown that learning actually unlocks new parts of your brain—meaning, if you stopped learning today, you would never know your true potential. You must experience new things to become more of who you could be.

Stay ready and alert—keep the curiosity of a student. Learning opportunities are everywhere, and you can learn from everyone. Acquiring knowledge tells your brain that you are worthy and worth investing in and builds your PWA.

Takeaway

Learning is good for your health. Learn something new every day.

#23 - Attitude

You can choose your response. Persist or quit?

Do you search for empty promises, mistakes, unmet expectations, and broken trust? An attitude of negativity can easily grow into a victim mindset—one that fills with despair, loses hope, and sees no personal worth.

Or, do you choose an attitude that equips you to face your challenges and persist through trials? A positive attitude can grow into a powerful accountability mindset—one that finds moments to be grateful, reasons to celebrate, sees potential, creates energy, and has cause to hope.

Again, you can't always choose what happens to you, but you can always choose how you respond. A positive attitude is only a thought away and can make large deposits in your PWA.

Takeaway

Equip yourself with a resilient attitude to weather the storm and overcome obstacles. *You* get to choose your attitude.

#24 - Routine

Consistency builds confidence.

Routines build familiarity. Familiarity builds trust. Trust builds confidence. Confidence can be banked and spent where needed. Routines can be simple or complicated. The "it" isn't as important as the execution and commitment to the routine.

Following a set routine not only strengthens your confidence but also increases your sense of peace and frees your mind to explore and solve problems.

Routines can be anything from how you mow the lawn or get to work, to where you buy your groceries or how you brush your teeth. When the action is committed to muscle memory, your brain is free to think or rest and both make great deposits in your PWA.

Takeaway

Find a routine that works for you and start yours today. Don't feel limited to one! Free your mind with a routine.

#25 - Environment

The places you live, work, and play effect your thinking.

When your basic day-to-day life activities are a struggle, you drain your resources and begin the race 100 meters behind the starting line.

Living and working in an organized environment, free of distractions, can send subtle messages that you are valuable and worth taking care of. As you begin to function with greater clarity and more efficiency, your PWA will increase.

There will always be something to clean, obstacles to overcome and less time to work; however, you can take steps to reduce the clutter, remove the obstacles, or change your location.

Takeaway

Clean up. Show yourself that you are worthy of a clean environment, worthy of a little TLC, worthy of starting at the starting line.

#26 - Fellowship

Everybody needs somebody.

Build a team and join someone else's team. A healthy team is vital to personal worth. Be sure to include these four key players in your fellowship:

Mentor. Believes in you and your potential. Helps foster growth by asking questions and listening.

Cheerleader. Encourages you in good times and bad.

Giver. Provides information, financial support, or tools with no conditions beyond your engagement.

Connector. Introduces you to people and opportunities. Promotes and advocates for you.

Takeaway

You cannot do it alone. Everyone needs help, encouragement, and an outside perspective.

Chapter 3

Empower

Empower yourself with opportunities to lead, succeed, or fail without self-judgment.

Empower yourself by taking ownership, staying committed, and giving yourself permission.

#27 - Flexibility

Be ready to adapt and course-correct.

Often we think changing course is equal to failure, inadequacy, or worthlessness. This could not be farther from the truth.

When you stand on intrinsic value instead of something external like success, circumstance, or appearance, you have the freedom to be flexible. Alterations in your plan do not equal failure or diminish your value. Instead, flexibility can help you grow in wisdom and allow you to thrive in changing conditions.

Additionally, as you become more flexible, you'll experience more peace. You'll become more comfortable solving problems and adapting to new circumstances. A flexible mindset can build your PWA as you adapt and persist in a changing environment.

Takeaway

Standing on intrinsic value allows you the freedom to move toward your goal, aligned with your vision, and make course corrections along the way.

#28 - High Hands

Personal boundaries are necessary for sustainability.

Boxing coaches say, "Keep your hands high." They say this because they don't want you to get knocked out. Punches make the highlight reel, but defense—"high hands"—sustain a fight and provide opportunities to deliver your knockout punch.

Attacks can come in the form of criticism, but also as demands on your heart, mind, body, resources, time, and talent. It's ok to say no, or put limits on what you commit to. It's tempting to give until you're empty, but you must set personal boundaries to stay in the game and make your giving sustainable.

Holding your hands high can increase your confidence, worthiness, productivity, efficiency, and creativity, as well as physical and mental strength.

Takeaway

You've got one life with limited resources. Treat yourself as though you are worthy of protecting— you are. Keep your hands high.

#29 - All In

If you want 100%-level results, give 100% effort.

In the circus, you have to go all in. If you were to cautiously jump from one trapeze bar to another, try to walk on a ball, or casually walk on a tight wire, you would fail. Commit 100% to experience success earlier and more frequently.

Making a commitment—being all in—helps you let go of the old familiar and firmly grab the future. You cannot grab the next trapeze bar without letting go of the first one.

Engage first. Honestly look at your talents, time, resources, opportunities, and tenacity. Then, empower yourself to pursue your passion. Go all in. You have a purpose. Find it, embrace it, and go after it! The world needs you to be you—no one else can.

Takeaway

You owe it to yourself to put your all into what you do. Don't be timid. Don't hold back. Engage and then be bold. Be authentic.

#30 - Weeding

Just because you can, doesn't mean you should.

There are many good things to do, but not all of them align with your purpose, passion, or skill set. Like weeds in a garden, these "good things" can sprout up quickly, consume all the nutrients in the soil, and occupy the best places for sunlight—effectively starving and crowding out the flowers you *want* in your garden!

A mind crowded with weeds can lead to exhaustion, lack of focus, depression, and hopelessness. Pull the weeds! Removing the "energy-drains" and "responsibility-hogs" will give your PWA fertile soil and room to grow.

Where are you investing your energy, time, talents, and treasures? Do they align with your core values?

Takeaway

Pull the weeds! Focus on tasks that move you toward your dreams and goals. It's ok to say "no" to distractions and say "yes" to you.

#31 - On Time

Arrive on time... or early.

Keeping a commitment to be on time is one of the simplest ways to make PWA deposits and one of the easiest to let slip. We are often late because we:

- Prioritized something or someone as more important
- Overscheduled
- Think, "It doesn't matter if I'm on time. No one is really counting on me."

When we are late, we rush, we spend energy unproductively, we feel bad, and make withdrawals from our PWA. When the account gets low enough, we adopt a victim attitude and identify as "always late."

Arriving on time can begin to rebuild your account. Let it become a habit that generates dividends for your PWA.

Takeaway

What prevents you from showing up on time?

#32 - Airplane Mode

Unplug to recharge yourself.

Prioritize yourself. Be present in your own life. Give yourself the same respect and attention that you would give to someone you consider important. If you don't, eventually you will burn out and crash. A car cannot drive on the highway at the same time it's in the shop for a tune up. Similarly, you cannot continue to work while you are taking care of you.

Schedule time for self-development. When you take the time for yourself, whether it's for exercise, time off work, or merely an hour of reflection in a park, turn off all devices. Paying attention to technology can sacrifice your "recharge" time.

Give yourself time to be unreachable. You deserve it. Only you can go on airplane mode, no one else will set this boundary for you.

Takeaway

Making yourself unavailable at times is not only ok, it is necessary to avoid burnout and maintain productivity.

#33 - Ask

Keep asking until you reach understanding.

Have the courage to ask questions and make significant deposits in your PWA.

When we stop asking before something becomes clear, we indirectly tell ourselves that we are incapable of understanding. Often we fear that asking questions will reveal our lack of knowledge and diminish our value.

We stop asking too soon because we don't want to appear foolish. But what is more foolish: Pretending to know but remaining ignorant or acknowledging that we don't know and relentlessly seeking to understand?

Takeaway

Be brave enough to ask questions until you understand.

#34 - Scribble

Sometimes we need to step outside the box, take a deep breath, and make a mess.

When you work between the lines, you only develop one way of thinking. Grow your perspective and color outside the box! Bend the rules. Get creative and give your brain a bath.

Scribbling stretches your brain beyond a rigid system of thinking, exposing you to new concepts and possibilities.

When you give yourself permission to make a mess, you allow yourself to see connections you couldn't see before. You can consider alternative perspectives and improve your ability to solve problems.

Takeaway

Give yourself permission to make a mess and have fun without an agenda or reason. Expand your mind by scribbling outside the box.

#35 - Today's Best

Yesterday's best is not the same as today's best or tomorrow's best. And that's ok.

Different variables lead to different outcomes. Everything changes—so don't condemn yesterday's best by today's standards. Or vice-versa.

As your energy, mood, opportunities, and resources change from day to day, so does your "best effort."

When you think you have performed beneath your abilities, be slow to judge and quick to gather information. Give yourself some compassion and understanding. Do the best with what you have today. No judgment. No criticism. Then do your best again tomorrow—whatever that may be.

Takeaway

Your best effort will change from day to day. That's ok. It doesn't mean you are lazy or a failure.

#36 - Enough

Know when to walk away.

There will always be imperfections. It's about doing your best for the day, finding satisfaction in your work, closing down a project, and moving forward.

If you aren't careful, the pursuit of perfection can grab you like a black hole. It can rob you of precious time, creativity, energy, resources, growth, and hope. Perfection is unattainable.

When you stand on intrinsic value instead of external value from success or failure, you have the freedom to give your best effort and move on. Give yourself permission to pursue excellence and avoid the trap of perfection.

Takeaway

Strive for excellence in your effort, not perfection in your product.

#37 - Break

Running on fumes is bad for the engine.

Breaks are as important as fuel, sleep, and vacations. Listen to your body!

Pushing beyond your limits to get things done results in bad form, frustration, and a feeling of inadequacy. Sometimes to take three steps forward, you must first take a step back.

Take a minute to slow down, step away from work, and have some fun. Recharge your batteries and your willpower. Replenish your creativity and return to your challenges with a fresh perspective.

Takeaway

Taking breaks can remove blocks to creativity and problem solving, reduce feelings of inadequacy, and improve your energy.

#38 - Jump!

Embrace your strengths. Grow and test them.

What are you passionate about? Where do your talents and skills lie? Accept them and develop those areas.

Test the limits of your strengths. Jump early and often while the long-term impact of a mistake is low. As you become more confident in your abilities and more comfortable in assessing risks and rewards, you can begin moving from the playground to the big leagues where risk and impact are higher.

Make PWA deposits by growing your strengths! Jump to the next level, find your footing and then jump again.

Takeaway

Take it to the next level. Invest in your talents, passions, and skills. Don't settle. Jump.

#39 - Mistakes

Mistakes are a natural part of life and everyone makes them. You are not alone.

Mistakes happen. It's a question of when, not if. You cannot eliminate or avoid them.

A mistake does not have to be a loss. It can be an opportunity to learn, gain new perspectives, and find your next challenge. If you want to see a mistake as an impassible mountain, it will be—but it doesn't have to be.

If mistakes are going to happen, why not take advantage of them. The more you face and learn from your mistakes, the more PWA deposits you make.

Give yourself the chance to succeed or fail without judgment. Don't let mistakes define you.

Takeaway

See mistakes for what they are, not who you are.

Chapter 4

Encourage

As you grow your PWA, you must continually fuel yourself with encouragement. Respond to thoughts of quitting, nagging doubt, feelings of inadequacy, or the encroachment of a victim mindset with encouragement.

Encourage yourself by shifting your perspective, developing personal motivation, and remembering your past victories.

#40 - Firefighter

You are a problem solver first, a (<u>fill in the blank</u>) second.

Problems are inevitable. They can pop up like small wildfires and raging forest fires. If you aren't ready to respond, they can consume you and your PWA.

Learn to be a professional problem-solver—a firefighter.

Prepare yourself to solve problems. Allow extra time for unexpected fires so you can put them out quickly and keep moving forward.

Equipping yourself as a firefighter can reduce the impact of expected and unforeseen fires. Additionally, problem-solving can make large deposits into your PWA! Every new problem has the potential to be another deposit.

Takeaway

We will always face problems, so learn to enjoy, and get good at solving problems. Embrace your inner firefighter.

#41 - Not me

It's not always about you.

Rejection can be overwhelming. It can appear as an affirmation of personal worthlessness and a reason to quit.

Your offer of help might be ignored. You might not get the new job. You may face criticism or abuse. Rejection can come as a roaring hurricane or a slow leak, but it does not automatically mean that it is your fault. It can come from someone else's past, preference or current situation. It's not always your fault.

Actors can be rejected because they remind the producer of an ex or the casting director couldn't wait to get to the bathroom. Maybe the director got distracted and wasn't paying attention or the producers simply had something else in mind. Often, the rejection an actor faces has nothing to do with his or her talent.

Don't assume blame, burden, guilt, or responsibility that isn't yours.

Takeaway

It's not always personal. Look around and see what else might be going on.

#42 - Affirmations

Encourage...yourself.

How many times have you said:

- "I'm not good enough."
- "I can't."
- "Why try? I don't have the skills, time, talent, etc."
- "It will never happen. I always mess up."

You talk to yourself every day. Words have weight and repetition is powerful. The more you hear something, the more you start to believe it. Do you send yourself encouraging or discouraging messages?

Instead of affirming a sense of worthlessness, use a helpful affirmation. Positive affirmations can reveal what's already inside you. Strengthen those qualities and make significant deposits in your PWA.

Takeaway

Your words carry meaning. Say it enough and you'll start to believe it. Choose positivity.

#43 - Self-Respect

Don't make fun of yourself.

Throwing yourself under the bus for a laugh is easy. It can appear to be humble and approachable, but too much self-deprecation can alter your self-perception and deplete your PWA.

Disrespecting yourself can unintentionally signal to others that they don't have to respect you either. This can grow into an echo chamber where you begin to hear your joke repeated in the words of those around you. In this manner, a joke can morph into a perceived truth—but it's not true.

You are a miracle. Countless events had to line up just right for you to be born. Countless more daily events have to occur for you to continue living. Treat yourself with respect.

Takeaway

Recognize your worth and show it through your words and actions. You are valuable. Be nice to yourself.

#44 - Forgive Yourself

It's okay to forgive yourself.

Self-forgiveness sounds simple, but it's one of the most challenging things to do. It becomes incredibly difficult when your mistakes are directly linked to your PWA.

It can be tempting to deny a mistake, run from it, avoid it, use it to justify self-punishment, or define yourself by it. However, none of these options are healthy or lead to growth.

What happens *after* the mistake is almost more important than the mistake itself. Like everyone else, you will make mistakes. When you make mistakes, seek to understand what happened instead of punishing yourself. Forgive yourself and stop the drain on your PWA.

Takeaway

After you make a mistake, choose self-forgiveness. Recognize that you are not the mistake. Be compassionate towards yourself and grow.

#45 - Pay Once

Acknowledge, own, accept, reconcile, and move forward.

Humans make mistakes. Unlike other creatures, however, we tend to remind ourselves of the mistake hundreds of times over—often years into the future.

Although repeatedly recalling a mistake can feel comfortable and familiar, it can bring its own set of consequences: An altered self-perception, a false identity, stunted growth, and large withdraws from your PWA.

Choose to acknowledge the mistake, own your part, accept any necessary consequences, seek reconciliation, and then move forward. Doing so will stop the withdrawals and make deposits in your PWA.

Takeaway

Do not let a mistake haunt you and overtake your entire identity.

#46 - Lens

How do you see your world?

Is your perspective half empty or half full? All bad or all good? Optimist or pessimist? When it doesn't go your way, do you see a loss or a lesson?

What lens do you use when you look at the world and your circumstances? Is the lens helping or hindering your growth?

Are you quick to connect dots and act on assumptions? Or do you put your emotions in check and gather information first?

GREAT NEWS! If you don't like your lens, you can change it! Change your reality by altering your perception of it and watch deposits flood your PWA.

Takeaway

Everything and everyone has a lesson. Make the world your classroom. Seek to learn.

#47 - Emotions

Feelings are ok.

Having an emotion is not wrong. It does not mean something is wrong with you.

If you allow your emotions to "drive" your actions, they can distract your mind and affect your body. They can even result in a physical ailment.

Instead of labeling them positive or negative, right or wrong . . . stop. Breathe. Take the emotion out of the driver seat and find out where it's coming from.

What expectation, desire, need, or want is being met or not being met? Your feelings are markers. Use them to discover essential information about yourself.

Takeaway

Emotions can be effective advisors but often make poor drivers. Take back control. Don't let "driving" emotions deplete your PWA.

#48 - It's the Audition!

Learn to enjoy the journey as much as, if not more than, the destination.

An actor will go to many auditions—sometimes hundreds before landing a role. If it's just about landing the role, actors can face a growing mountain of rejection that can become debilitating and make significant withdrawals from their PWA. With this perspective, fewer risks will be taken and auditions can start to look more like obstacles.

An acting teacher once said, "If your goal is to perform, you must see every audition as an opportunity to do just that, regardless of the outcome."

Embracing the audition process can bring its own joy, freedom, and a positive attitude to an otherwise hostile environment. Indirectly, that perspective can help you win more roles as you relax and bring more of yourself to your auditions.

Takeaway

The journey is in itself an opportunity to live out your purpose. Don't miss the joy it has to offer.

#49 - Yet

It's not over ... yet.

Most things in life take time and are worth the wait. Few things happen overnight. Hold on. When you are tempted to give up, use your secret super power—the power of YET. When you face challenges, don't give up—persist.

DARK SIDE: The unsatisfied workaholic. Focusing on the end goal in excess can rob you of presence, blind you to daily realities, tax your PWA, and reduce you to a machine.

LIGHT SIDE: The patient optimist. Remembering that things take time, but also remaining present to reality can foster patience, forgiveness, joy, and peace. It can grow your PWA.

Takeaway

Remember that there are twists and turns, ups and downs to every journey. Don't let a moment define the experience. Hold on. Don't give up. Persist. You're just not there ... YET.

#50 - Celebrate

Make the journey more enjoyable with celebrations.

Consider a half-marathon. Along the course, people shout encouragements, applaud, offer water, and sometimes pass out energy chews (small, sweet, nutrient-rich snacks designed for quick absorption by the body and immediate impact).

These can make all the difference. The chews, water, clapping, and encouragement all drive a runner toward the finish line. Each one hits the body with another shot of energy and inspiration to keep going. Celebrating the mile markers makes the challenges of aching muscles and mental roadblocks more manageable. Reaching the finish line becomes more probable.

What keeps you going? What motivates you through pain and keeps you committed to the process? Reward yourself with celebrations. Your PWA will thank you!

Takeaway

Celebrate throughout your journey and at the finish line! Make the race enjoyable.

#51 - Record

Remember your accomplishments. Write them down.

A victory can yield positive, healthy fruit both now and in the future. Don't let a success go to waste by forgetting about it. Write it down!

Challenges, problems, and trials can seem overwhelming and impossible. When you face them, remember and draw strength from the mountain ranges you have already overcome. It can stop the withdrawal from your PWA and begin making significant deposits. Look at all you have already accomplished!

Write down your victories and look at them periodically. You'll get a high return on past investments. A quick reminder of past success in the midst of a current trial can be a significant boost to your resolve.

Takeaway

Remember your past victories to help sustain you through today's challenges.

#52 - #WashYourBrain

Remember who you are and that you have intrinsic value that cannot be lost, stolen, or increased.

You hear these messages every day: "You need the latest gadget." "You need to live there," "You are not enough." The list goes on and on as if these things will finally make you worthy.

The truth is, you are enough. Your internal value will never diminish or increase. It is always enough, but your perception of it can change.

Every day you wash your hands and brush your teeth because they get dirty. Don't forget to wash your brain too. Keep it clear of lies. You have nothing to prove. Live in that freedom. You're worth it.

Takeaway

Your internal value does not change, but your perception of it can. Remember who you are, that you are significant, and that you have value.

A final note from Jeff

Love of art and people led me to a career in entertainment. Unfortunately, my need to earn value and prove my significance turned performing into my identity and an emotional roller coaster. My personal value was directly linked to my successes, failures, appearances, and circumstances.

When I realized that I had intrinsic value that could not be lost, stolen, or increased everything began to change. It brought me hope, peace, joy, and the freedom to be present. As my perspective of personal worth improved, so did the quality of my work and my personal relationships.

Please keep this book handy and refer to it whenever you feel anything less than valuable, whenever you start comparing yourself to others, whenever you feel overwhelmed with criticism, or whenever you are tempted to give up.

Let *Blueprint For Value* be an inspiration to take back control of your thoughts and feelings. May it serve to remind you of your limitless value so you can get back to pursuing your passions and fulfilling your purpose.

You are enough. You are worth it. You have value.

Next steps

Share your story

I would love to hear from you! As you practice the habits listed in this book, please share your journey with me! Let me know how things are going.

Email: mystory@blueprintforvalue.com

Join the conversation

If you have habits not listed here that should be considered for inclusion in future books, send them my way!

Email: myhabits@blueprintforvalue.com

Dive deeper

For access to deeper exploration of these habits, visit:

https://www.blueprintforvalue.com

About the author

Jeff Koziatek is an inspirational speaker, certified life coach, and an award winning, international entertainer.

Organizations continue to seek out Jeff's creative talents to inspire their employees, entertain their guests and educate on a variety of topics, from leadership and teamwork, to communication and GRIT.

Jeff has spent more than 2 decades working in the entertainment industry. He has managed national touring acts, performed over 4000 shows, produced award-winning films, and operated a complete event management company.

He believes in the inherent value found in each person and his passion is to empower and encourage others to be their best selves.

Jeff is happily married to an amazingly talented and caring woman, and the proud father of two brilliant and creative young men.

But wait, there's more!

Inspirational speaker

To book Jeff for an engaging, interactive, entertaining keynote presentation that your guests will still be talking about weeks after your event, visit:

https://www.coreauthenticity.com/speak

Certified Coaching

For more information on executive coaching, creating culture shift, and individual coaching, visit:

https://www.coreauthenticity.com/coach

Notes